Southern
Messenger
Poets

DAVE SMITH, EDITOR

USELESS VIRTUES

USELESS VIRTUES

poems

T. R. Hummer

Louisiana State University Press
Baton Rouge   2001

10   09   08   07   06   05   04   03   02   01
5   4   3   2   1

Designer: Amanda McDonald Scallan
Typeface: Janson Text
Printer and binder: Thomson-Shore, Inc.

Library of Congress Cataloging-in-Publication Data

Hummer, T.R.
   Useless virtues : poems / T.R. Hummer.
      p. cm. — (Southern messenger poets)
   ISBN 0-8071-2668-3 (cloth : alk. paper) — ISBN 0-8071-2669-1 (pbk. : alk. paper)
      I. Title. II. Series.

   PS3558.U445 U84 2001
   811'.54—dc21

                                                                           2001029418

The author is grateful to the editors of the following periodicals, in which some of the poems herein
first appeared, sometimes in slightly different form: *DoubleTake:* "Surgical Lyric," "Telepathic Po-
etics"; *Five Points:* "Blood Oranges," "Erotica," "Little Epic of Oblivion," "Ring Cycle," "Sunrise
Raga with Cat Motif and Continental Drift"; *Kenyon Review:* "Antimetrical Lyric of the San
Joachin," "Encoded Dithyramb," "Mimesis," "Soft Money"; *Paris Review:* "Nietzsche in Bed: A
Translation"; *Quarterly West:* "The End of History," "Rotary Blades, Inc.," "Unfinished Eclipse,"
"Vocalese"; *Shenandoah:* "Catachresis of the Blade," "Elemental Fable," "Gnomic with Temple and
Ashtray"; *Southern Review:* "The Dredges," "Half-Life Study #1–5," "Useless Virtues"; *Western Hu-
manities:* "Domestic Lyric."

The author owes thanks to the Virginia Council on the Arts for an individual artist's fellowship that
assisted in the completion of this book; thanks also to Garrett Hongo and David Baker for careful
reading, incisive critique, and encouragement.

For Theo
For Jackson
and
For S.

Why Being or some other capitalized word? God *sounded* better. We ought to have kept that one. After all, shouldn't reasons of euphony regulate truth-functions?

— *E. M. Cioran*

CONTENTS

III. Axis

IV. Telepathic Poetics

V. Surgical Lyric

Coda

Useless Virtues

USELESS VIRTUES

At midnight in the backyard hot tub,
    pleasantly drunk, three old friends argue
One more time the meaning of *The Book of Job*.
    Floating in brothel-scented foam
Under California constellations, it is easy
    to picture the Man of Suffering, the whirlwind,
Dead cattle, the warehouses of the snow—
    especially the warehouses, which have vast
Quartzite double doors, where helicopters
    of ethereal whiteness enter and vanish, hauling
Neither suffering nor glory, but only another
    disgusting winter day for Moscow or Trenton,
Stoic taxis rusting through generations
    of storm-sown salt. It is about the moral
Evolution of the idea of God. It is about
    the survival of its own obdurate narrative,
Which could rescue even us nonbelievers
    from easy sentiment. It is about nothing
Except the incommensurability of everything,
    the shitty drama of pain that stretches
From Behemoth down to the structure of the atom.
    Nobody agrees. Even God refuses to be God
But breaks down in a windy turbulence.
    More wine. And the three of them lean back,
Watching lights sign the absolute sky, where,
    as though all human consciousness were forming
One vast, slow thought, the dream of the Cambodian boy
    on a red-eye flight to Dallas interweaves
Baseball, temple bells, roadkill, cemeteries, bread,
    sexual ambiguity, and a poster of Pol Pot nailed
To the wall of a compound, monsoon-faded, laced
    by bullet holes. The image comes through
This clear, this real: a yellow-and-black spider
    makes its decisive way across the vacant left eye

Of the dictator, which has been precisely punctured
      by a round from a surplus M-16. Meanwhile,
The 737 that cradles the sleeping boy reclined
      in its blue-striped seat threads darkness between
Los Angeles and Albuquerque, vapor trail
      a strand of invisible web joining the strafed
Face of the moon and an H-bomb test site.
      Everyone on the plane is sleeping, even the pilot,
Like God, oblivious at the switch, and all the people
      oblivious to his oblivion—otherwise
They would wake up screaming sensibly.
      But everything riding the sky tonight is silent.
Leviathan tortures Orion bloodlessly, and the great
      Eagle Nebula, screwing stars out of twisted nothing,
Is twenty-three trillion miles of decorum. Still
      the cattle are dead, the children are dead,
The body is pierced with cankers, and, on every horizon,
      snow masses its chronic obedience.

I

Domestic Lyric

Domestic Lyric

He washes the dishes. He does the laundry,
    bleaching by hand something delicate
And white in the bathroom sink. He sits

    at the kitchen table reading. Nothing of her
In the house but a resonant emptiness. A garbage truck
    shifts gears in the vacant morning street,

While a hundred miles to the east, the Atlantic
    eats into its own shoreline
Until whole streets of overpriced oceanfront

    split-levels begin to collapse. *I'll call*,
She said on her way out the door. That
    was years ago. As decades develop, he feels

The quality of his ignorance grow richer. Wars
    come closer. He hears cannons in the mountains,
The scream of a horse with shrapnel in its throat,

    the guttural thump of an Anglo-Saxon axe
Splitting a shoulder bone. He stirs a pot of soup,
    adds lentils and pepper to taste. He shuffles

A stack of mail: her boxholders, a magazine.
    At the moment his death arrives,
He is polishing silver: a stylized effigy of the sun.

    She wears it sometimes as a pin,
Or makes a pendant of it—either way he can see
    his own face distorted in its brilliant thorax.

There is fire, a famine, continental drift.
    The garbage truck grinds again.
Even dead, he remembers to lower the toilet seat

and check all the locks. *You look younger*, whispers the priest.
I am, he wants to answer, tracing the small prints
of a woman's hand in dust on the sarcophagus.

HALF-LIFE STUDY #1

A handful of powder can break a city's back,
     a scatter of sleet, cloudlight, luminescence of salt.
At the taxi stand, a driver from Senegal practices
     thinking in English. *Etoile*, he whispers. *No: star.*

Star, snow, diesel, moon, fatherland, wing,
     and the mystical incantation *carburetor.* Inside, beyond
Plate glass, a man and a woman stick in the throat
     of a life, in the gut of an argument, and one girl in pink

Is possessed by the Demon of the Grecian Urn.
     Atlanta airport: Every snowbound flight shuts down.
Nobody's going anywhere. Bursts of bar conversation
     syncopate into sniper fire: *Nice little culture*

*You got here. / If God intended folks to fly, we'd be born
     with more reservations.* Dangerous vortices of rage
Burn on Doppler screens. Everyone here wants transcendence.
     No life in the moment. Bodiless lift. The lyric's

Poisonous glow. The father of the girl in pink
     feels the ticket in his jacket pocket discharge
Its singular pulse of frustration. The mother breathes
     on the window and draws a cartoon face that fades

As she watches. Through its left hemisphere she silhouettes
     the taxi driver against his yellow rime-scummed Ford.
He, in turn, remembers the face of his own mother transfixed
     in the doorway the morning he took the road to Dakar

And the rotting shipyard. Then the sick grind of ocean. Then
     the convention center. She is still standing there,
Expressionless, almost swallowed in empty shadow.
     She will never move again. *United*, he thinks, *Las Vegas*, meter

Not running, each snowflake a punctuating loss.
Coca-Cola. Please direct me to Peachtree Street.
Multiple avenues to salvation. De-icer. What's your angel's name?
Whiteness fouls every access road in sight.

ELEMENTAL FABLE

Because he lost his keys, his house
    closed its mind to him.
He stood on the porch in moonlight,

    humiliated. To be canceled
By one's own possessions: insufferable.
    But what could he do?

The house was old, brick, barred:
    impregnable. He had made
Sure of that, at considerable expense—

    steel storm doors, dead bolts,
Encoded security—all to keep everything
    safe, and now look: the furniture

Turns against him. Urinating
    in the yard, beside the shadow
Of a gatepost, he suddenly hates

    the very idea of Neighborhood
Watch, everyone indoors with dishes
    and sofas, observing this twisted man

With his cock in his hand in moonlight
    at 2 a.m. Down with the bourgeoisie!
And yet he would sell his soul to know

    what happened to that miserable
Key ring. He zips himself, and there is the sound
    of the body bag in it,

The nameless one found extinguished
    in the gutter on Exile Street,
His death an irrelevant puff of wind,

a little inconvenience
For the cop who makes the call
   thinking of home at the end

Of his shift, an easy chair, a little music
   on a cheap stereo.
Pity me, great ones, for all I want

   is the affection of a couple of objects,
Some vases, a beat-up table, all arranged
   so I can see them through the frame

Of a black marble lintel as I enter that old address
   which, when I have to go there, will
Open for me lovingly, oblivious to the moral.

ROTARY BLADES, INC.

From the window of the train, she sees the sign
    on a warehouse, enormous and crude,
Like something painted by a hyperactive child:
    Rotary Blades, Inc., permanent, yet looking as if

It could vanish any second, which it duly does.
    She watches orchards disappear, wheat fields,
Pickups, silos, ashamed of how her mind runs
    in its tight, deadly circle like every other mind:

Brown light forklifted out of the wrecked shell
    of a depot, sepia refraction under a pier,
Opalescent sunrise an elegy for color over a sudden
    silvery bay. She dreamed her lover

Was lobotomized. He could not speak, but there he was,
    alive, in the angular world again, stumbling,
Staring at things. She woke so quickly it shocked him
    back into nothingness. Incision should always happen

On a foggy morning, the door to whatever
    you care to call it opening almost invisibly
In a pearly ambiance. At the next stop down the line,
    conductors make bad jokes, and there are junkyards

And trailers along a little river, as if people actually live there,
    but the train moves on, the blades turn,
There is blood in the air, an omnipotent brume of shit.
    The dream lied, but his brain did break.

Surgeons whispered, and he vaporized: sun on fog, on wind.
    Did I say lover? Husband, then. First one,
Then the other, then a desperate face in some dream
    of an afterlife so false it might as well be endless.

OLIVE BREAD

He needed flour, so he pawned his trumpet.
    He needed salt, so he sold a pint of blood.
In an alley near the market, a stockbroker bought
    his wristwatch. It was raining, and the pantry roof

Had sprung a leak. He counted his loose change slowly,
    standing in the shadow of a newsstand, next
To the *New York Times* and the hulk of a gutted Volvo.
    He read a headline. Thunder. The air tasted of gasoline.

He needed water. And olives—good black Greek ones cured
    in their own oil. But where the hell
Can you get such things in the middle of a war zone?
    There was a remote golden color in the sky

He'd never seen there before. When the smoke cleared,
    the city yielded a poisonous odor of yeast.

Blood Oranges

They are eating blood oranges
    on the broken fire escape.
Blood oranges—what makes us want
    to say that? A boy and his mother,

Quietly eating blood oranges.
    Behind them, in the apartment,
Another china plate smacks against the wall.
    The last plate, the mother knows.

She's been counting. Next will come
    the soup tureen, gravy boat,
Heavy serving dishes. The boy drops
    bits of peel into the alley underneath.

Two stories down, they detonate in afternoon light
    while ice on the pitted iron grid
Of the platform implodes inversely.
    At least she has saved the one bowl,

This one, where blood orange segments lie.
    Who knew her grandmother would leave
Her this? Who knew how the war would end?
    Inside, the husband comes to salt

And pepper shakers, not so easily broken.
    He throws them again and again.
Bone china. Blood oranges. In this moment
    the names are sacramental,

A domestic transubstantiation. The boy
    looks out into the contusion
Of the gathering sunset and kicks
    the ladder of the fire escape,

Years since rusted through.
  He learned this from his father,
As he learned in school *Of all the beautiful*
  cities on Earth, the most beautiful is ours—

As he learned from God the blood
  of the orange is the blood of God,
The ice of the fire escape is the ice
  of God, the growing darkness

In the alley is the darkness of God, growing.
  It is winter and God is cold.
From the northernmost province of Paradise,
  he can hear the apartment wall

Shattering saucers and cups. He almost
  remembers that anger, or something
Exactly like it. The innocents. A bowl
  of blood. The jawbone of an ass.

Ring Cycle

At the crematorium, the story goes, they gave him
    the ring he had bought for her,
White gold with constellations of tiny diamonds,
    a row of square-cut sapphires
In a black hole at its core. What would he do

    with it now? At home he opened the urn,
Dumped the ashes on the kitchen table, buried
    the ring at the place where he set
Her plate so many mornings—all gone up
    in a greasy smoke now, into

The disinterested abstraction of sky.
    When they cooked together, she loved
Complex flavors, Oaxacan moles with roasted tomatillos,
    deep ragouts of winter roots, cardamom, dark sauce
With garam masala. Often when he thought of her,

    it was as a visible aroma of ground
Coriander and allspice. He touched the stove,
    touched the iron pans on their hooks,
The sieve, baker's peel, baking stone. He brought down
    bottles from cabinets, bundles of dried herbs

From the pantry, fresh ones from the crisper drawer.
    He dumped everything on top of the ashes.
With her scarred wooden spoon, patiently, he stirred
    white peppercorns, turmeric, rosemary,
Spanish saffron, blending carefully with carbon,

    teeth, and the irreducible bits of bone—
Then took it up in double handfuls, threw it
    into the ceiling fan, closing his eyes, breathing.
It's like all your stories, she said then, giving him
    her characteristic sidelong smirk:

Sentimental and thin. You're absolutely right,
    he answered, *as usual,* blinking at the nebulous
Sparkle on her finger while he sat
    finally down beside her the way
He always did, taking the proper fork.

II

Erotica

EROTICA

Even here, where there is still a shining
    on the surfaces of buildings, on rivets, bindweed,
Jar lids, asphalt—here, where you can still recover
    harmonics spun off augmented chords
Ambulances improvise after midnight down

    by the warehouse as workers on graveyard shift
Hoist crate after meaningless crate off pallets
    and back again: or here, where starlight bothers
Construction sites (so stubborn, so permanent)

    and abandoned wrecking balls revolve
Spontaneously, touched by that larger revolution—
    or maybe that never happens; is it only
Gossip?—and here, where when the insomniac
    looks out the window of the room

Where she lives on sufferance for a life or two,
    she sees the same impossible hungers
Endlessly piling up: gin bottles digging in,
    medical bills refracting out-of-tune faces

In the backs of bars where stockbrokers play
    a subtle music nobody really wants,
While invoices fatten, and the luminist moon
    uncovers the shocking, beautiful curve
Of a forklift's roll bar—somehow, yes, even here.

HALF-LIFE STUDY #2

She lies in bed in a strange city, watching
    her lover while he sleeps, someone else's
Books on the shelves, strangers' snapshots
    framed on the bureau: a coal train
on its track along a river fixed in black

    acid against limestone—a Toyota
At curbside, fading, releasing its ghostly odor
    of bromide—anatomy of branches
Through a window, smudged against pale sky.
    She is living in an old photograph,

A fin-de-siècle tintype, brown-edged, slightly
    out of focus. When the sunlight
Makes its way across the comforter to touch her,
    she feels herself begin to disappear.
Her palms go first, clarifying like lenses. Then

    her legs—daguerreotype of a wartime amputee.
Chemistry is merciless, her aura helpless
    in this light. When the man wakes,
There is nothing beside him but a face, oddly
    faded, familiar in a distant way—

An ancestor maybe, distorted behind old glass
    in a gold-foil frame—or nobody,
A child in a porch swing who never had a name,
    never had a life, not even forgotten, regarding him
With a crudely fixed gaze, colorless but certain.

GNOMIC WITH TEMPLE AND ASHTRAY

While they were making love, it crossed her mind
    that she could kill him. Easily. Quickly.
He was so helpless there inside her, making
    his little moans. She could kill him

Or not, while morning gathered brilliance
    east of the factory tower. She understood
The cool clarity of that vaulted air. She loved him
    terribly, but she could do it

With the ashtray, maybe, a heavy crystal thing
    full of lipsticked ashes and cotton balls
Already stained nail-polish crimson. A stroke
    behind the ear. As he kissed her shoulder

And she watched the pulse in his temple,
    an enormous neutrality came over her.
There was nothing personal in it. When he died,
    it would break her heart.

Yet she could do it now, as easily as that
    luminous little cloud beyond
The smokestack she saw out the window
    lifted its weightlessness in the light.

MIMESIS

The fat sun of Atlantic autumn burnishes equally
    the gold leaves of a ginkgo and a police cruiser's chrome.
The officer by the fender is dressed in silver and black,
    leather and steel, insignia of rank, light body armor

In homage to Egyptian foot soldiers, samurai, all
    the great forgotten infantry of Troy.
The young man facing him is dancing—if dancing means
    moving with great care to the rhythm of a moment.

The officer leans forward, the smaller man leans back,
    matching him inch for inch. The officer moves
His right foot, the other moves his left, his T-shirt
    suddenly a false skin sutured with sweat.

The sun makes no distinctions. The sun does not divide
    epic from tragic, gnomic from dithyrambic.
It sheds the luminous fragments of its dying godhead
    equally on the frog and the fireplug,

The cathedral and the whirlwind. I stand at the crosswalk,
    my arm linked in a woman's arm, though no one
Is there. The cop cocks his head to the right, the perp
    cocks his to the left at an equal and opposite angle.

If he could only become the other, he would vanish
    into the safety of a badged chest or the vaulted chamber
Of a Smith & Wesson .45. Sun in my eyes. The tear
    of the great release. *Shadow your enemy,*

The martial artists say. *Become the mirror.*
    Reflect the swordless sword. When the music starts again
The dancers bow, then shimmer into the counterpoint
    of selflessness, law, the lyric of likeness, which is love.

Death's-Head Love Lyric with Aftertaste of Anise

The French Quarter tarot-reader
    told them *Love finds a way;*
Cross the great water—a blessing and a fortune,
    and they paid her. Then, rain

Locked in over Melpomene Avenue
    past midnight, as a tractor-trailer
Groaned, double-clutching its cargo
    of mint Chrysler hearses out

Of some fogbound industrial warehouse
    and north toward the Causeway.
Lake Pontchartrain parted at the touch
    of those headlights to let

The exiled ones pass. This woman and man
    had come together here
Out of mutual kindness, driving state
    after state to leave the Atlantic

In its blackmail behind them. They wanted
    to turn every darkness that ocean
Could raise against sky to nothing
    but an accidental residue of the story

Of their lives. But at this corner bar,
    a little Pernod drinker sat
At his usual table alone, laying out,
    beside the napkin into which he coughed

So delicately, his worldly goods—
    pocketknife, key ring, cigar case—
Then staring at them all, as if considering
    the final pincer move

In a private ritual chess game. They watched
    his consumptive grimace
For any foreshadowing of their grace.
    Outside, the avenue darkened—

Not toward the absolute, but into
    a blueblack translucence, the lip
Of the world's shadow brushed
    in clumsy passion against

The scarred forehead of a hurricane.
    He sat sipping his poisonous drink
And pondering the pattern. And if
    he sat that way forever,

Who would show the dead their long
    way home—to Hoboken, to Fargo?
Who would the stillborn have left to trust,
    if not this pastis-desiccated man

In his moleskin suit, spreading
    liver-spotted hands, then lifting his glass
And setting it deliberately down, as he might
    the black rook that ends

One more player's gambit? The man and woman
    turned from his omnipotence.
They ordered him a sacrificial drink. They paid
    another bill and stepped out

On the avenue, which instantly lifted them
    on a murderous gale off the lake
Into an aurora of gas-well methane.
    The man at the table raised his snifter

Toward the window as they drifted,
     his face of an interrogating angel
Darkening through rain-sheeted
     plate glass to one last drop

Of licorice-shaded blood hawked down
     from the heavens over streetcar tracks
And pool halls, voiding along
     the cathedral's dome and into a sea of fire.

SOFT MONEY
10/31/97

An American moon tonight. It renounces its own
    definition. It lights the sidewalk cinematically—
Scatters dramatic chiaroscuro, as if a war is imminent,
    as if this nightclub's façade conceals a resistance cell.

And don't we love the moon in wartime, isn't the brownout
    seductive, the wound, the disguise? On the corner,
One man is dressed as a freedom fighter. He tells
    an endless joke to his brother the bombardier,

His comrade the amputee. It is late October,
    almost time for the millennium to turn
Angelic. That's a kind of punch line. Children appear
    in sheets, ghosts from a pogrom, laughing.

Then everyone stands aside for the woman in white—
    white gown, white mask of pheasant feathers.
She scatters the crowd and it loves her for her violence.
    Hers is the only real secret here: what she has endured

At the hands of what officers, on what islands,
    in theaters of combat so remote from us
That even the newspaper pales. In the nightclub
    they are playing blues, the 99th empty chorus

Of *Stormy Monday*. A sailor orders a Manhattan,
    and the Nazi bartender stabs a cocktail onion
As the doors swing back. She enters, a windy zeitgeist.
    All intelligence ceases. The teletype clatters into silence.

Here in my chains, in my scars, I might be anyone
    dressed as a quaint communist or shell-shocked exile.
How is it possible to be this powerfully in love
    with nothing but a moment? I will take my chances

With history, I will lift my hands and beg,
    I will die in a nameless trench with a hole in my throat
You could drive a half-track through. There is moonlight
    translating the silent battlefield into a city

In eastern North America. Across the street, on the wall
    of a bombed-out supermarket, someone has painted
A crude S, like half of a child's swastika. I know
    this woman in the white dress is beyond me.

I see her as if through the window of a troop-train
    where men sleep in an exhausted aura of sweat.
She is standing on the platform of a station in the heart
    of the country, holding her mask in place against the wind.

If she spoke, we might recognize her voice,
    give her a name and forget her, but her camouflage
Is impenetrable. She opens a white beaded bag,
    pulls out a handful of bills. She could own us all.

ANTIMETRICAL LYRIC OF THE SAN JOACHIN

One syncopation in the clean rhythm of another
    enjambed morning, November, 6 a.m.:
A switch engine slows by the depot, and two men

    swing off. They walk the strophic walk
Of fathers in their early forties who still have pity
    on the work of the brake shoe and the piston.

The only exegesis they want now
    is oatmeal at this diner built in the shadow
Of a smokestack capped by methane flame.

    I watch the woman at the grill sling hashbrowns.
She cannot forget the nakedness of junkyards
    along the highway west of Modesto,

The paternal violence of the wrecking ball.
    She believes in angels she saw once
In the backyard of a tract house in Bakersfield

    next to a blocked-up Impala with hellfire
Detailed on its fenders. Her memory splinters
    the otherworldly prosody of their moaning.

But crossing-arms ascend, and the switchmen
    open the door. Over eggs, I consider how language
Refuses the fault lines that grind between

    the dactyl and the trochee, the cries of cherubim
Screwing in a shadow cast by General Motors. And what
    does her Father in Heaven whisper through the hot grid

Of the window screen, hand lost in the caesura
     of his greasy fly? *Say nothing. Tell no one.* You want
Sausage or closure? The check. All right. Scan this:

     Breakfast is not iambic. Neither is mercy.

VOCALESE

As he is talking long distance, his lover slips in
    and hands him flowers, tulips
In cellophane, a dozen red, a dozen yellow. Six

    states away, his wife does not register the threshold
In his voice, a swift grace-note of difference.
    The children have sent her roses, Mother's Day

Bouquets. Both have called. Cincinnati, D.C.—sunlight
    on the patio is nearly Grecian in its purity.
They talk quietly, old friends, while the lover waits

    with perfect patience in the bedroom. All morning
The oceanic feeling drove them. In a marginal depth of sun
    filtered through clouds and a window shade,

One told the other, *Look, for you I destroy my history, my gender,*
    my skin. Beyond the dooryard, I imagine, deadly nightshade
Droops in wisteria shadow. The lover has removed

    T-shirt and jeans. In the other room, the one
Voice laughs quietly. Something is being said in the classical
    key of domesticity. They tell each other everything. The lover

Lies down naked on the bed, wondering at the normal
    sound of a single larynx. He loves the husband
Who forgives himself on the far side of the wall.

    I recognize all this from the distance of the dark tower,
From the other dimension of a pillar of smoke, a pillar of fire,
    a cloud in the shape of the absolute. It could all be simple:

If the receiver falls, if the day goes on, two bodies could be burning
    identity to a fine white powder. Coffee would brew
In the kitchen, lilies on the table lean toward compost. But

I was born in another life, believer, and I will die there
     in the sunlight maybe, on an ordinary day
In May, having sent my mother flowers, having heard

     a saxophone *a capella* on the stereo, the bent blue-notes
Of a mountain jay in the ash tree, or the beautiful hiss
     daylight makes destroying itself against prisms, wind-chimes,

One lover whispering the name of the murderer of God.

III
Axis

Every inquiry is a seeking. Every seeking gets guided
beforehand by what is sought.
— *Martin Heidegger, 1899–1976*

In Memoriam CVH, 1921–1994

1.1 — *in which he is extinguished*

Nothing in the blood, nothing in the brain,
Nothing in the tongue contains us at the end.
How was it this man died? Completely.
He breathed into concealment. Or concealed
His way into unbreathing. He was and then
Was not. Even a death can be normal, common.
Even a death can feel familiar. He turned unreal
As I watched him. Right in front of me

He transformed himself into an ordinary shadow.
And that was a death to die for: transparent, compact,
Unbeautiful but unassuming. Almost abstract.
His lyric ended. He was just a dead man now,
Untouched by starlight, storms, wings, scythes, harps.
His last words were *I want to be a corpse.*

1.2 — *in which he is created*

In the idea of the past, on the threshing floor
Of history just south of the primal hut,
A grandmother throws down her bushel of sorry wheat.
Around her a luminosity of motes—above her
A kind of solitary weather we have forgotten how to name,
Grim in its atmospherics, bearing the bruise of God
From sky to river to face to stone to colorless cloud—
And behind her an evolution so heartless it had to become

The story of what passes for destiny among the blesséd.
Unthinking, she scatters her grain; unthinking, she murders
An age of the world. All this for a little flour.
All this for a loaf of chaffy bread. She threshes.
And out of the dust and sweat of her filthy labor
A shape appears, which she slaps into breath: my father.

1.3 — *in which he denies himself*

This child is a disbeliever. The motherland
And fatherland never did those things to each other.
Awful things. Awful bodies. He understands
He came from somewhere. But if love negates the lover,
Why be here? If he ran away from himself,
It would all still be as lovely as it is, the wheatfield
Would go on ripening its floury half-life,
The forest grow darker, its creatures more richly concealed

In the absence he would leave behind.
Poor little childless father. He wants to wipe away
Memories of scenes he never saw. He wants to unremember
The trench he crawled out of, the unmothering machines
That convoyed him down from heaven the day
He invaded this dimension and declared himself a war.

1.4 — *in which he is clarified*

To the east of him, therefore, a phalanx of tractors
Advances, camouflaged against the margin of the forest—
To the west, threshers triangulate the torn theater
In which grain blitzes its fated ripeness
Out of the ground of its own being, and retreats.
Nothing is neutral, not sweat, rot or erosion.
His enemy creates him. A V-formation of geese,
A platoon of cattle: everything is explosion,

No no-man's-land. And as for his childhood,
His orders are clear: you can have it as long
As you can hold it. Mother and father and God
Are good, but something familiar and wrong
Breaks holy ground in the blood.
He prays to his Father in his mother tongue.

2.1 — *in which he receives a designation*

From the other side of the earth, in the Holy City
Of Thought, the Philosopher of Being regards
My tiny father through the transparent indeterminacy
Of a glittering logical lens inflicted on him by the gods.
Turning it awkwardly and squinting, able to measure
The child's position that way, or else his velocity—
First one, then the other, never the two together—
He begins the outline of a hypothetical biography,

Or hagiography perhaps. Here is a boy
Born in ignorance, stunned by Being, thrown
Out of nowhere into the center of a horrible story
Being written around him in blood, by no one.
The Philosopher smiles. His inquiry is plain.
At the top of a fresh page, he writes my father's name: *Dasein*.

2.2 — *in which he is eclipsed*

On the Continent of the Philosopher,
The Axis is revolving.
Or the Continent resolves around it:
This problem needs either solving
Or ignoring; the Philosopher is unsure.
And he is distracted. Heavy machinery
Grinds in the dark outside the city gate,
And smoke obscures the scenery,

A novel, insidious smoke.
Surely it has a source. Perhaps the trains.
Trains are everywhere now, a mechanical vermin,
Like the laundry truck at the corner, like the tank
At the city center. Much is obscure.
But the obscure fascinates him. That, at least, is clear.

2.3 — *in which he is possessed*

His jacket is tweed but cheap and worn.
It is cold in the city, and the soldiers are a problem
Of an unphilosophical nature. The Philosopher could have sworn
By the age of thirty he'd have arrived at the apophthegem
That would summarize the cosmos. Matters stand otherwise.
Matters, in fact, are disastrous. Writing comes slow,
Thought slower still. The meaning of the universe
Does not quite *elude*, but exacerbates his mind somehow,

While the Meaning of the University has grown as obvious
As the nose on the face of—well, one of *them.*
Time to get on with it. Time to take care of business.
But this perfect, ignorant boy in his brain—what to do with *him?*
The market is full of soldiers. There are tanks at the edge of town.
Time is getting away from him. He scowls and jots that down.

2.4 — *in which he is defined*

In the deepest, most numinous, most inaccessible space
Of mind, the Philosopher apprehends that very Being
Of which he is the Philosopher: my father's intaglioed face,
Rising up as it does all unexpected and glowing
With intention out of concealment. It implies
Nothing less than everything. So much labor
Of the spirit for something so elemental? Yes.
All over the Continent, the perimeters of the coming war

Appoint themselves. There is evidence: black stacks
At all points of the horizon belch indelible smoke.
What are they burning out there? the Philosopher asks.
But this he does not write. His work,
He intuits, is Other. The conquest of Otherness.
This genius is a bastard? This bastard is a genius.

3.1 — *in which he reaches a limit*

Dasein cannot dream the Philosopher. All Being long
He will never think this thought: the dream can dream
The dreamer dreaming. The boy he is belongs
With the animals; the man he will become
Belongs among men. It is simple that way, and clean.
Only in one's mother tongue can one express one's own
Peculiar hatred. His is of the elements, of carbon against carbon.
He is already growing into it. The pure machine

Of conscience will roll over him and he will not recognize it.
What passes in him for innocence requires another definition,
A new hierarchy of spirit. But no one dares devise it.
He is the minister of compost; he is the eggshell king,
Commander of lyric droppings, master of decomposition.
Like a good boy he does his chores, unconsciously uncomplaining.

3.2 — *in which he is conceived*

Father is a form. Forgetting this,
We utter him at our peril.
Likewise *sun*, a brilliant, imperious
Form, almost—but only almost—indestructible:
For *God* too is a form, and *peril*, and *forgetting*,
Water and *war*, *animal* and *Dasein*.
Likewise everything you can think of: penetrating
Form, like a bullet in the brain.

Utter him, then, and risk your life: a war
Becomes my father. He is still a tiny form,
Insignificant. He is crossing the great water
In utero at the age of twenty, waiting to be born
Heroic, monstrous in his mother's blood, to save
The world. Or at least to be born alive.

3.3 — *in which he is illuminated*

In the middle of an ordinary midnight, in the middle of an ocean,
Dasein leans on a ship's rail and lights a Lucky Strike.
Match-bronzed, he is simply himself, a self-authenticating
    phenomenon
Etched in scrubbed brass and khaki, backlit, moonstreaked,
Handsome as a filmstrip, a military classic.
He thinks precisely nothing. There is nothing to be thought.
That is the beauty of it. What is, is. The ship's wake
Glows cinematically, a sentimental symbol shot

In black and white and set beneath a headline.
He has come out of concealment and is lingering here.
He has a purpose. He is full of intention,
And his body is bright with it. You can see it in the way the moon
Arcs the filmy emptiness above him. He is the luminous center
Of the world beyond the birth canal. Speak, friend, and enter.

3.4 — *in which he becomes the word*

My father's language steams across the ocean,
A mechanical fogbank of suspect rhymes: *human,*
Hydrogen, broken, noun, bone, machine.
It is returning to its homeland to investigate its own
Caesarian beginnings. Knife in the belly. Bloody origin.
It wants to kill. It wants all compromising information
Dead. Otherwise, what *is* a mother tongue, a nation?
Its syntax beats in the heart of the ship, a passion

For form that would murder its own son,
Then invent the word *sacred* to explain what it had done.
But my father on the deck requires no explanation.
Holy war, cleansing war, genocide or revolution,
It is his. His mind is his language, but a war
Is circumstance; it demands its metaphor.

4.1 — *in which he is betrayed*

The Philosopher sits at his desk in his underwear.
Rain on his study window deposits a residue
He's never noticed before. He observes in wonder.
What is the Being of rain? Once he thought he knew,
But something in it now reminds him curiously
Of that little colleague—what was he, a theologian,
A Kabbalist?—who came with his hat in his hand, desperately
Asking a favor. Impossible to grant it. And then

The man vanished as if he had never been.
He and his whole family. Rumor had it they'd taken a train
Somewhere into the heartland. Never heard from again.
Pleasant little fellow. Rumor had it he played the violin.
Turned into smoke right there on the threshold: vaporized.
Nothing left but his hat, which is just the Philosopher's size.

4.2 — *in which he is obscured*

The Philosopher scorns such phenomena. The Axis
Is his concern. What sits at the Center of Being
Governing Being's revolution? Whatever it is,
He will name it. It is there, just beyond his perceiving.
The Axis is time. The Axis is not time. The Axis is the margin
Along which the war between humanity and God is fought.
Being turns on the Axis; the soul is the heat of its friction.
Or: the Axis impales the world, and the world spins, caught

On a core of pure, dispassionate pain. But another thought
Disturbs him: has the Axis vanished—eroded,
Absconded, collapsed? Or perhaps it *never was*? Still,
Something turns us. And language alone is not
The Axis. It may have another name, but it is *there*: corroded
By God's neglect or human error, but provable, real.

4.3 — *in which he is completed*

Now the great ship brings *Dasein* ashore.
He walks the plank and sets foot on the Continent.
He is ready. This is his personal war.
He is being born for it. Nothing can prevent it.
Does the air resist his approach? Does the Continent tremble?
Who can tell? When *Dasein* takes one step,
An artillery shell dissolves a cathedral.
Another step, and a tank platoon blows up

An orphanage. Thus, inch by inch, his advance.
Thousands vanish, revolved into concealment.
Dasein waves them on. Their Axis is a circumstance
He can do nothing to help them circumvent.
Dying's not so bad, the joke goes, *just don't be
Around when it happens.* Bombs fulfill that prophecy.

4.4 — *in which all is explained*

And everything will remain—that's the mystery:
Whole cities untouched, whole continents undisplaced.
Beyond the ordnance and the massive machinery,
Everything that is happening is merely commonplace.
The armature of the pelvis funnels one human into Being,
And another, and another. That much, the Philosopher understands.
For the rest of it, who cares what God is doing?
In that question, philosophy ends, and begins.

Stones forget about blood. Blood washes away.
The wind is less than nothing, a nerveless gas. And dust—
What is dust? Trash that makes you sneeze. A cheap cliché.
Why worry that the rain is full of it now? All of this
Is error. The Greeks would agree: the real remains
Real. The rest is explosion, artillery, the rattle of trains.

5.1 — *in which he is abandoned*

The Philosopher dresses himself. He has someplace to be,
An appointment, a rendezvous. His whitest shirt
Calms him. He admires it. And his very expensive tie
Was a gift from someone important. But what about this hat?
He holds it, undecided. It reminds him of something unpleasant,
A half-remembered dream. He looks around himself, about to leave,
But something holds him. The flat is perfectly neat,
All the appliances silenced. It's foolish, but he's ready to grieve

For the books arrayed in their perfect jackets, the papers in piles
On the desk, even the clean drapes. How strange, how irrational!
He wants to tell the piano he'll only be gone for a little while—
To another city, yes, a distant country, really nowhere at all. . . .
On the sidewalk, the rain lets down its bony grit.
It's good that he has his hat to protect him from this shit.

5.2 — *in which he reads* Being and Time

Dasein arrives, expected, at a certain city, in a certain street.
He makes his way through the impure sunrise to a certain door.
It opens at his approach. He enters, confident
That this is the moment he spent so long being born for.
The hat rack is empty, of course. He searches the unpeopled rooms
Following that great sound he hears—foyer, parlor, kitchen,
It grows louder, an immortal golden hum
Like the sound of a galaxy of bees, or an immaculate machine

Stamping the face of God out of immortal alloy.
He finds it in the study, under the books, piercing the floor, the desk,
The ceiling: an antimatter shaft or negative axle, cusp
Around which the flat, the world, is spun—climax of the story,
Axis at last, grinding, numinous, omnipotent.
Dasein studies it, frowning, then finds the off-switch and flips it.

5.3 — *in which he vanishes*

Time to die. Something in his brain
Dictates it. Some grubby little führer
In the genes gives the order
And the synapses fire. Bedpan,
Morphine, scalpel, hearse in the rain:
Details merely. I see my father
Turn to ash, or turn the corner
At the end of the last street in the city of *Dasein*.

He turns his back. Away. He prepares
The corpse within him, and then becomes it: *turns*
Into it, as we say. Our words turn on us. Crematoria burn
Discreetly in our cities. He would have it so: no stars
Obscured by his rising, no carbonized trace
In the weather of his stillborn, unimportant face.

5.4 — *in which he becomes an apologia*

So the end of history comes, and nothing happens.
The landscape goes on, oaks beside trenches beside sheep;
Morning shows up in the cities; the markets open;
Children stumble to school, shell-shocked by the usual sleep.
Railroads keep their schedules; conductors erase
Certain recent destinations and begin speaking kindly
To the passengers again. Churches forgive even the priests—
It is worth any price to have an ordinary Sunday

With the ordinary sins committed and confessed.
We converse with each other again, just as we had done—
Well, always really. Has anything intervened?
There are fewer of us now, but surely there always have been.
Here and there a crater—hospital, house, mysterious ruin—
But we have jobs and gods again; we are serious, and blessed.

IV

Telepathic Poetics

TELEPATHIC POETICS

To enter them all in darkness, over and over, coming
    through rear windows or baffled front-door locks,
Not worried about patrol cars or neighborhood watch, subverting
    streetlights, yard dogs, flowers or any lack of flowers:

To touch whatever is there—jewelry, shells, old letters,
    broken combs, dirty rag dolls, a saxophone on a stand—
Tenderly, as if to steal but not stealing, indiscriminate,
    while the righteous married breathe each other's sleep

In adjoining bedrooms: all this trouble just to be somewhere,
    anywhere, among furniture however polished or broken down,
Among bills, bank statements, death certificates (but none of them
    stamped with our names): in extinguished basements

With fuse boxes, rusted switches invisible but offering
    at least the possibility of ordinary light.

Half-Life Study #3

When she wakes one morning, *Mood Indigo* is playing
    on the radio at the back of her mind.
Rain blows, too, in distant courtyards, its small music
    sharp against deserted benches and quartz-
Veined flagstones. In the steeple across the boulevard
    it touches the chapel bell. Resonance. *Mood Indigo*:
Behind the ballroom door of the medulla oblongata,
    all the dead musicians lift their nerveless horns.
Or is there just a radio after all, sitting on a hallway table—
    a mahogany RCA with an incandescent dial
The lovers forgot when they went downstairs to mix
    another gin and tonic in the kitchen? No matter.
The horns stay lifted. And the syncopation of rain plays on
    against the window of this room where other instruments
Measure the rhythm of her blood, the strange counterpoint
    of cell against cell. Nurses' carts. Interns humming.
So many years that scalpel and ether can't control
    take shape in a nonexistent saxophone's bell.
She could make a theory of it, or at least a religion,
    if she could only move her hands again.
Trombones in a garden. A set of drums in the bedroom.
    Behind a curtain, lovers forgetting to breathe.

48

THE END OF HISTORY
4/23/94

An ordinary apocalyptic morning
    in the Americas—no earthquakes, no asteroids,
Just the benevolent shadow of a broken promise
    of rain. The adze of Pacific wind
Hones cumulus clouds to nothing. Or does it
    work the other way? And all the newspapers
In the supermarket agree: RICHARD NIXON DEAD.

    The gears of identity turn slow,
But the mesh is implacable. Gone under
    the bonewheel, that spectacular ego, sucked
Down the augers of the absolute. I am choosing
    the best asparagus, I am buying olive oil,
And somewhere that Plasticine face, disturbed
    by a permanent stubble, is growing

Even more inhuman. Yes, he was a private citizen,
    yes husband and father, yes nothing more
Than carbon, oxygen, hydrogen. But against
    the overblown blue screen of memory
Napalm flares up on every channel. Bombs
    go off in the vacuum tubes of Saigon.
It is a spring afternoon in liberal Oregon,

    where skinheads shoot stained glass
Out of the façades of synagogues.
    I am writing a check, I am pushing my cart
In a contemplative way through the parking lot.
    I remember that twisted little figure
Beside Mao's ghost in the shadow of the Wall.
    Eisenhower. Kissinger. Hiss. I will not give in

To the fragmentary, I tell myself at the stoplight.
    I will make my language whole. I prepare
A simple pot roast, I scrub the toilet clean.
    Friends come by for dinner, stepchildren
Of clarity, hunted down by the obscure.
    By midnight, I am almost asleep, almost ready
To dream again of our common disaster,
    the ratchets of expediency tightening I-beams,
Stroke, stroke, stroke, in the spine, the brain, the heart.
    Time to reinvent humanity, I am thinking,
Time to retool the scrotum and the womb.
    Liar, what do I know, and when
Do I know it? It will be the monotonous
    nightmare again, a thunderhead with the profile

Of a weasel breaking up—or, stalled in the market air
    above us all, one crow blacklisting the wind.

UNFINISHED ECLIPSE

Penultimate light: no asylum. I try to imagine consciousness
    without identity—a cloud without a sky—
And, as at the sound of a whiplash or an institutional bell,
    I stand, brushing hair back from my forehead, to stare

Stupidly upward, where the sun has begun to tarnish.
    Blinded beside my lawn chair, I want to make a list
Of everyone I might ever love, to picture all
    their faces and hold them in my mind at once,

But every time I assemble them, there is no room left
    for myself. There are children, grown, with their own
Sorrows and polymorphous joys, unplanned
    and incomprehensible except for being abstractly human.

And my imaginary sisters, my unborn fathers, my other
    passionate selves, who were they again? They appear to me
As a multitude in a stone-walled compound, imprisoned there
    by priests—these masturbators, slow learners, the left-

Handed and otherwise inspired, summoned for saintly prayers
    and trial by fire, snake pit, or mercurial water,
Made nameless through their common losses. Flowers
    grow carefully against the backyard fence where I hold

The pinhole camera: columbine, poppy, the sacred lily
    nuns terrified into purity generations since. This is one
Ordinary day in a life that suffers no more than the ordinary
    sorrow. Somewhere down the block

There is a muffled hammering. Up the street a mower
    meditates, a ripsaw founders. The morning deepens.
But that filth in the courtyard corner, the twisted one
    who drools crystal into the alyssum: that man

Almost has my eyes. Sooner or later this world will begin
 to make sense to us: like music, perhaps, peculiar
At first, then trivial in its beauty—or the hands of a husband,
 inevitably once a stranger's. Light is merciless,

Like healing. There are welts from scourges, scars
 from leeches, lesions at the ankles from irons.
There is lilac on a trellis. And in the course of things,
 the moon orbits in against the brilliance.

Encoded Dithyramb

He sits on the bridge-rail at midnight, watching
    silhouettes of helicopters eclipse
Star after star over the river, spotlights probing

    for a speedboat-load of cocaine runners
Or the translucent body of a drowned girl, sunk
    or floating, tangled in a queenly trail

Of brocade and foam. That morning, he saw
    the first narcissus blooming
In sunlight on the boulevard, between a soup kitchen

    and the vacant Masonic temple.
Invisible pulses, transparent symbols, flooded
    the traffic zone, broadcast from satellites

Over the Egyptian heads of concrete lions
    set at the boarded-up gate
Of the holy of holies. But now the river conceals

    its mudbacked inventory of relics,
Its secret handshake. Through the fifty feet of darkness
    his legs dangle into, under the bridge

Where homeless women keep house in the shadow
    of a concrete buttress, the gods have grown
Opaque. He stares down, but nothing

    gives him back his face. He thinks about this
While searchlights avoid him. What else
    can he do? He thinks about it.

Nietzsche in Bed: A Translation

At that critical moment, she whispered later, the panic
    of absolute doubt breathed on her left breast
While he was touching her right: what if this light reflected
    in the window, this candle smoke, this empty
Water glass, were neither something nor nothing
    but a deadly coupling of the two,
                      radiating
Cancerous phosphorescence in every atom,
    photon, and cell of the body of the world?
He knows that when she came, her face fixed
    in the ancient gnostic gaze of ecstatic horror
Of being. Her voice drew him into her
    with an irresistible undertow.
                    The chambers
Of her memory seemed dark at first. Then he saw
    shapes giving off a little neon luminescence:
Distant figures, a landscape maybe, or a city street
    in the 1950s, a mother, a dog dead
At the bottom of a canyon, broken glass on a sidewalk,
    a fist, a cul-de-sac. Later,
                  after her riptide
Washed him out, and the night resumed its steady state
    of traffic noise and clicking of thermostats
In the comfort zone, he picked up the book one-handed
    from the bedside table and looked again
At that fierce face on its jacket—apocalyptic mustache,
    lidless eyes darkened over
                  with impossibility
Of mercy—and it seemed in the lamplight their bodies
    shifted genderless toward translucence,
These histories into a single sadness beyond the blind
    alley of the opposites, aphoristic, subterranean,

Their palms on each other's bellies undermining
the immortal rupture

that breaches flesh and story.

SURGICAL BOMBING: HORIZONTAL LYRIC

Turned on their sides this way, the houses
    look like fragments of a crystal lattice

Or an unchained double helix, the structure
    of everything shifted ninety degrees

By some impersonal god or bored disaster.
    The woman wants to know everything

About them suddenly—the same houses
    on the same street she has walked

For years, incurious. But who put that icon
    in the second upstairs window? Who

Painted the near façade that poisonous shade
    of green? Who made the soldier in the street

A perpendicular invasion? And that gable—
    she wonders what architect imagined it

Just that way. How did the carpenter feel
    with his oiled saw and ball-peen hammer,

Dangled that far from the sidewalk, which, oddly,
    was to his left this time? And when the surgeon

Lifts the dome of her chest away, he discovers
    a deep-cut valley in the body's cavity

Like a relief map of the ancient Indus, where the river
    of the spine lays down its timeless track

Through the forest of the ribs, the caverns
    of the small intestines—a poisoned landscape,

Villages razed or burnt, irrigation pumps dismantled,
    fields sowed with quicklime, spearheads

And salt. The surgeon makes a note—*internal
    accident, massive*—and catalogs

The tracks of plundered oxen leading off
    beyond the arched skull, what remained

Of the belly's granaries, the bins once bursting
    with pulses torn and scattered now,

Vaulted aqueducts emptied, the sacred fouled
    Precincts of the ventricles, red-caped

Infantry and their ammunition belts, a woman
    screaming in the market place: stripped,

Mouth open, waiting on her back
    for the necessary end, the bloody stroke.

Sunrise Raga with Cat Motif and Continental Drift

Another dawn unconstellates the sky—another sun reborn
    to replace the one we loved and then mislaid.
That's how the cat in the window thinks. All cats
    are Egyptian in their odd moments of enlightenment.

In another house, a girl in a hallway sits patiently on her chair
    watching a beam of sun broaden through the fanlight.
Or is it the dust in the air she watches—motes, fractal flakes,
    cat dander suddenly luminous there before her?

She is neatly dressed and pretty and well behaved.
    In school, she is a proven learner of facts. Facts define her
And she loves them. But now, it is wonderful to her
    that a little uncleanness fills the air with beauty.

To the west, at the end of a block in another city, a man
    on a bus-stop bench remembers the farm
Where he was born, dawnlight over wheat, wheat dust
    revolving its blinding globe around the combine

Those distant July mornings. The office where he works now
    is a clean, filtered place, a little like a hospital
With its antiseptic smell of deodorant and ink. All the forms
    he reads and stamps concern accidents, claims

And counterclaims. A woman dies in an elevator, a car
    is flattened by a train. There are codes for all these things,
Regulations and procedures. He knows them. Worse,
    he understands them—more than he understands

How the woman sitting next to him acquired precisely
    that feline gesture, or how he himself was given
Skin, teeth, hands. A little light reflecting from a sports car
    blinds him. *The sun again*, he thinks, and lets it go.

In his lap, a slick magazine he bought but will never read
    conceals a photograph of a Hopi priest on a mesa ledge
In Arizona where he goes morning after morning as he has done
    since the beginning, to sing the song that brings

The light. It will not come without him, or without
    the anthropologist who stands next to him
Taking notes in the predawn cold, or the cameraman
    who waits, wanting a cigarette more than anything,

Even more than he wants the sun to hurry, to hear this
    Uto-Aztecan riff and rise, releasing him to his Jeep
And his little flat in Phoenix, where certain women come and go.
    The priest, dressed in jeans and a flannel shirt

With a little dander on the sleeve, lifts up his arms and freezes
    into an archetype. The camera clicks and he is standing there alone,
Mouth open, as the dawn releases itself from the emptiness it requires,
    catlike or heartless as any god, toward nowhere and beyond.

V

Surgical Lyric

Biographic Lyric

Out of their chemical union, his obsession.
    Out of their oblique pleasure, his perverse joy.
Out of their pattern, his pattern. Or: the starry lathes
    revolved, and turned him out,

Polished and shivering, from a bar of solid carbon.
    Each night, moonlight retreated as he followed
His own animal scent from bank to barber to table,
    shedding bits of skin, walking upright

As best he could, distracted by the fiction of the human.
    Meanwhile, it rains. I take out the garbage.
Someone I love is angry and shouts a little.
    The neighborhood cats walk secretly, wrapping

Their skins tight around the ember of their destiny.
    The rest of the mystery is immaterial.
Whatever else he does in my life, I offer you this.
    Except for the nightmare, it is most of the story.

Passion Play with Residues of Carbon

Downriver, where the rain stops falling suddenly
    in the middle of the night, unnoticed by anyone
But the lovers, factory smokestacks lay a darker darkness
    over the face of the water. *Darker darkness:*
No judgment in those words, just a pure description,
    inadequate as the phrases *Whom I loved* or *In the beginning.*
There had been a problem with the chemical balance
    in one of the factory vats, some uncertain concern
About the rising water. But the longed-for disaster
    never came. And the rate of violent crime
Was in decline—about that, everyone agreed. Now
    the moon appears again through the clouds'
Corrosion, disclosing the river channel to the man and woman
    on the bridge. Holding hands, they gaze
Into the sudden nightscape, reading in its reflectiveness
    the entire periodic table. They turn to touch
One another's chemical faces. But what is their revelation
    to us? We hover at a predetermined height
Over the country, over the earth, precipitated into sheer
    statistics, brooding on the invisible fate
Of the elements. Everything rises here—in post-storm mist,
    in the body. *Whom have you loved?* she might be saying,
Or *Whose side are you on?* Who could possibly answer?
    Nothing left but to release a liter of night-birds
Into the apparatus, increase the concentrate of moonlight.
    Stars break through, no one knows how many.
Let them enter the formula of river. They keep it trembling
    where we want it, under the useless bridge.

HALF-LIFE STUDY #4

He remembers the little train
    in the beautiful country—
Massed green of forests, stone-lined
    fields, then apricot trees,

A wooden pen, a goat. Villages.
    Larkspur. A small
Iron footbridge over the tracks.
    And on a garden bench,

Asleep, intricately folded in
    on herself like a Swiss
Army knife, his mother the eight-
    armed goddess. Today

He sits alone in the curry shop
    trying to read the news.
Blowing rain against plate glass:
    hours, and nobody comes

For pakora, vindaloo, aloo saag.
    An ambulance screams past,
A Volvo, two starving dogs, a bearded
    holy woman with a sign

In illegible French, magic
    marker words half destroyed
By weather. Wiping a palm
    on his white chef's coat,

He thinks of the land scrolling past,
    his father vigilant
At the third-class window.
    Groaning and rattling,

The train made its dark incision
          in the belly of the world.
He was only a boy, dressed in his best
          white suit, sucking cheap candy.

What could he do against the anesthetic
          green of an alien country?
His life is not a bad life now.
          On his wall one Jesus,

One Shiva, one Buddha. It is
          his life. Nothing in it
Shames him. But he must not forget
          his father's eyes seared

With intelligent sadness.
          And when he thinks
Of his mother, it is necessary to see
          the eyes of a goat—

Gold flecks against darkness, weird
          vertical slit of pupil
Intent on dangerous difference—
          and the anonymous look

On the face of the goddess as she lifts
          the animal's chin to bare
The throat, the impersonal bléssed knife
          borne suddenly down.

CATACHRESIS OF THE BLADE

For days the scar aches, the spot
    on the left side of her chest
Where the knife went in. It makes

    no difference that trees
On the boulevard open against
    façades of brick rowhouses,

Or that the moon these March evenings
    is dimly haze-ringed,
Its grottoed face half healed.

    Walking home from the market,
Carrying a little food, she hurts precisely.
    You might imagine the weapon

In various ways: a bright steel blur
    under streetlights, carved
Bone handle stained with palm-sweat,

    or something heavier,
Bayonet, machete, nameless blade
    from a forgotten city

Buried seven levels and two millennia
    in its own dust. The ache
Is flawless, the scar immaculate, token

    of a wound that was
A work of art. Geraniums bleed
    in every flower box she sees.

The world, she knows, is perfect,
   because the gods
Who do not exist put a heart in her,

   and then, with a single
Invisible stroke—power, glory,
   mercy—they cut it out.

THE DREDGES

Then there is another astonishment:
    the smell of the memory of sweat,
Residues of sunlight on sheets, the lovers' bodies
    glowing with spindrift and salt.
I think of these things in Bellingham,
    where the elemental suffocation of rain
Obscures asthmatic dredges working over
    Puget Sound. Sooner or later it all surfaces,
Silt, old metal, mussels. Subscendental dragnets
    lift everything back. This present
Is a ghost of disaster. Afterburn of sunrise
    on the cliff face rusts the edge
Of Europe, already blunted against Washington's
    oily rock. You can taste the bile-
Slick rainbow of history on the cold
    Pacific spray. In that bedroom
We were more merciful, whoever we were.

    I had come to you with nothing,
Not even the lyric of my life. It was afternoon,
    and the angled light revealed
One body above another, identity
    eclipsed in the labor of equalization.
We were churning in the riptide
    of a new paradigm, ageless, genderless,
Where the center of beauty defines itself against
    the drag of the solar plexus. Endless,
The mediation of the ferries shifting tourists
    from the quay to the roulette wheels
Of Lummi Island, where the Reservation goes on
    winning back the stolen propositions
We sum up in the word *America*.
    Those blue boats vanish in a cloudbank,
Rain clarifying losers' windshields.

But the dredges keep heaving their hulls
Against the Sound, wakes white
    in this ore-colored light. They broadcast
Spearheads and rotted pottery, tires, alluvium of lava.
    Anonymous, they love the water
With a higher passion than any yet spoken of
    in compromise—no language known
For the story of what comes back in the strain
    of cable, ligaments, skin gone
Colorless in the touch of afternoon light
    through plate glass where you took
The namelessness I brought you, one body,
    one sex, everything dragged up
And examined in the enjambed brilliance
    we were becoming, tidal and unlonely.
South of Bellingham, where I drive empty
    in the rain, I could envy God's oblivion, except
For the shape of a hand on the wheel, and the breath
    of the fogbound horn taking over
The radio—jazz FM from Seattle, "But Beautiful"
    closing the skyline down.

Surgical Lyric

Because this is the binary universe she thinks—created
    of equal light and darkness, energy and matter,
Everything by halves, everything revolving—she has bled
    continually from March to May, sometimes heavily,
Sometimes only spotting, distracted by the difference

    between wholeness and hemorrhage, pressure
From inside her own penumbra. She receives the sacrament
    of a hysterectomy. One IV spins her
To the other side. Anesthesiology is a philosophy:
    it divides the general from the local;

It denies so many narratives that cannot be spoken,
    illegal sentences, paradoxes of pure syntax
That might destroy nations, syllogisms that break
    paradigms down to bases, to salts. This is one year
Beyond her lover's death from cancer of the breast.

    This is two years after the divorce. Her doctors
Are innocent here, their faces full of boredom
    and wonder. They know the tradition.
They never look back. Underground, chemistry works
    its transformation: light recedes, shuts down.

You could say it was the whole dome of starlight
    razed from the firmament, or the tipped
Leaking uterus cut from the belly of Andromeda and thrown
    into an antiseptic bucket. Therefore, everything now
Is secrecy. Everything is code. Every word is written

    by a prisoner in a cell, on toilet paper, scratched
In ink distilled of blood from a dirty incision. Every image
    is a dangerous message, propaganda disguised
As description of the moon, horrible and deadly

political information twisted to look like metaphor.
Confession? The opposite of confession. As her breath now
    where the nurses sterilize themselves is the opposite
Of breath. And can't you remember how you touched me
    that night by the river, let's say, while we looked
For the Pleiades? They were gone from their place

    behind the constellations, every lying cell
Of their faint blue light cankered with absence, and darkening.

LITTLE EPIC OF OBLIVION

Certainly there was a river. There was a boatman, the smell
    of wet wood, a relentless music of oars.
Now, dusklight gives up worrying the little room where he lives

    with his razor and his mirror.
Out the window, nameless stars begin appearing. He ignores them.
    He ignores the rusted fence and the overgrown lane.

He misunderstands their nature. They were something to him once,
    as the moon was something to him,
And his hands, and a river. And certainly there was a woman,

    dark-eyed, imperial, with a birthmark
On one arm. He ignores her photograph. He ignores
    her shape beyond the window

Where she kneels picking herbs in starlight. God-drenched
    and -dominated darkness hangs
At the edges of his vision. Maybe he was powerful once,

    maybe even beloved. Mistakes were made
And they struck his memory blind. What were their names,
    the winged ones who cut him down?

It seems to him he was somebody then. His shaved face
    is vaguely familiar. But when he sets
The razor down, nothing connects him here. He was betrayed.

    He betrayed himself. There must have been
Tactics and lies—there must have been monstrous battles,
    spear wounds, screams, puking,

Dishonor, dust. But certainly a river. The woman beyond the window
    is dark-haired and kind to him. He turns

His back on her. He ignores the belt of Orion, the prophesies
    of television news. He wants to get back
The goat's blood someone gave him—how it trembled in its wooden bowl
    as that stranger stood before him saying *Drink*

And remember, and he drank—how it tasted of wild garlic
    and bitterweed when the woman touched
His face with her brutal small hands and he loved her forever.

Coda

HALF-LIFE STUDY #5

Just as the rain begins, a man dressed as a priest
    steps out of a café doorway onto the sidewalk, moving
As if there were no such thing as weather, down the avenue
    where shop windows display all the worldly goods
We are told we must give up. A priest, or a man
    dressed as a priest? Rain, or chemistry dressed as rain?
Hands invisible in his cassock sleeves, he walks without looking
    left or right or even before him, head down
In an attitude of brooding or meditation or constant prayer.
    He passes the boy with no legs singing for coins
In the shadow of a shoeshop's sign, the woman in mink hiding
    her face indignantly from the rain in her priceless collar.
Emblems are everywhere, and he makes his way among them
    respectfully but with determination, as if his lifelong training
Were in techniques of proper relation to surfaces and their meanings.
    Suppose he carries a copy of *The Cloud of Unknowing* wrapped
In bookshop paper hidden in an inner pocket? Suppose
    he carries a copy of *Das Kapital*? The café waiter
Deferred to him, brought him an extra serving
    of excellent bouillabaisse with honest peasant bread.
The soul of a priest is nothing to a waiter, as long
    as the food is free. The waiter's mother was a beauty
In her youth, took many lovers, died embittered and faithless,
    broken by loss of face. No one to blame, no one to forgive.
Memento mori are worth whatever price. Now the waiter clears
    the table, lifting saucer and soup bowl, brushing crumbs away.
No tip. His reward will be beyond the surgeon's shop, the brothel,
    the Temple of Apollo, in the fogbank at the avenue's end.

"Useless Virtues": *The Book of Job*, 1. 18–19: "While he was yet speaking, there came another and said, 'Your sons and daughters were eating and drinking wine in their eldest brother's house; and behold, a great wind came across the wilderness, and struck the four corners of the house, and it fell upon the young people, and they are dead; and I alone have escaped to tell you.' "

The Book of Job, 38. 22–23: "Have you entered the warehouses of the snow, or have you seen the storehouses of the hail, which I have reserved for the time of trouble, for the day of battle and war?"

"Olive Bread": *Essentials of Classic Italian Cooking*, Marcella Hazan (Knopf, 1992).

"Gnomic with Temple and Ashtray": *The New Princeton Encyclopedia of Poetry and Poetics*, ed. Preminger and Brogan (Princeton, 1993).

"Death's-Head Love Lyric with Aftertaste of Anise": Napoleon House, Chartres Street, New Orleans, Louisiana.

"Soft Money": Richie's Pacific Bar and Grill, West Broad St., Richmond, Virginia.

"Antimetrical Lyric of the San Joachin": *Meter in English: A Critical Engagement*, ed. David Baker (U. of Arkansas Press, 1996).

"Axis": Martin Heidegger's reputation as one of the greatest philosophers of the twentieth century rests largely on his first book, *Sein und Zeit (Being and Time)*, published in Germany in 1927, which takes "the Meaning of Being" as the terrain of its inquiry and *Dasein* (being-there) as that inquiry's focus. For Heidegger, *Dasein* is "an entity which does not just occur among other entities. Rather it is ontically distinguished by the fact that, in its very Being, Being is an *issue* for it." Furthermore, "*Dasein* is not only close to us—even that which is closest; we *are* it, each of us, we ourselves. In spite of this, or rather for just this reason, it is ontologically that which is farthest." *Being and Time*, trans. Macquarrie and Robinson (Blackwell, 1962), 32, 36.

In recent years, abundant evidence has proven that Heidegger was a Nazi—a party member who was for a time put in charge of the restructuring, along party lines, of the German university system (see, for instance, Victor Farias's *Heidegger and Nazism*, [Temple, 1991]). In this fact, obviously, lies the nub of an ethical conundrum for anyone interested in Heidegger's philosophical work.

"Half-Life Study #4": The Wee Curry Shop, Glasgow, Scotland.